smoothies
& juices

simple and delicious easy-to-make recipes

Christine Ambridge

p

This is a Parragon Publishing Book
First published in 2003

Parragon Publishing
Queen Street House
4 Queen Street
Bath, BA1 1HE, UK

ISBN: 1-40542-533-4

Printed in China

Produced by the Bridgewater Book Company Ltd.

Photographer Calvey Taylor-Haw

Home Economist Michaela Haw

NOTES FOR THE READER

- This book uses both imperial and metric measurements. Follow the same units of measurement throughout; do not mix imperial and metric.

- All spoon measurements are level: teaspoons are assumed to be 5 ml, and tablespoons are assumed to be 15 ml.

- Unless otherwise stated, milk is assumed to be whole milk, eggs and individual vegetables such as carrots are medium, and pepper is freshly ground black pepper.

- Recipes using raw eggs should be avoided by infants, the elderly, pregnant women, convalescents, and anyone suffering from an illness.

- The times given are an approximate guide only. Preparation times differ according to the techniques used by different people and the cooking times may also vary from those given. Optional ingredients, variations, or serving suggestions have not been included in the calculations.

contents

introduction

What better way to use the variety of exciting fruits available today than by whipping them up into a delicious smoothie? Juices have also experienced a revival in popularity recently, and are an excellent way of extracting the nutrients of vegetables and fruits.

Try to have a supply of frozen fruit at hand, such as bananas, strawberries, and peaches. To freeze bananas, peel and slice them, then freeze the slices in a single layer on a tray before transferring them to freezer bags. You can do the same with small chunks or slices of other fruits. Always have a supply of ice at hand, too.

An electric juicer is not essential, but if you own one you can enjoy nutritious juices in their natural state. To give you an idea of how much you will need in the way of "raw materials," 1 lb 2 oz/500 g of apples yield a scant cup of juice; the same weight of blackberries yields 1⅓ cups. For vegetable juices, 1 lb 2 oz/500 g of carrots yield a scant cup; the same weight of tomatoes yields 1⅓ cups.

A food processor or blender will take a lot of the work out of preparing these drinks, and will ensure that they are mixed to the right consistency. Finally, don't forget to have a good selection of glasses and straws ready!

guide to recipe key		
	very easy	Recipes are graded as follows: 1 pea = easy; 2 peas = very easy; 3 peas = extremely easy.
	serves 2	Recipes generally serve two people. Simply halve the ingredients to serve one, taking care not to mix imperial and metric measurements.
	10 minutes	Preparation time. Where chilling or cooling are involved, these times have been added on separately: eg, 15 minutes + 30 minutes to chill.
	10 minutes	Cooking time.

pineapple tango
page 16

summer fruit slush
page 44

smooth nectarine shake
page 56

iced citrus tea
page 82

smoothies

Smoothies are a delicious way to enjoy fruit all year round. Whenever you have a surplus of fruit, instead of reaching for jelly recipes, why not set some aside for drinks? Simply prepare and freeze them in the usual way (see page 4), and you will have a constant supply of frozen fruits ready to use for drinks at any time of the year. This is an ideal way to enjoy fruits, even when they are out of season.

forest fruit smoothie

		ingredients
extremely easy	1 ½ cups orange juice	DECORATION
	1 banana, sliced and frozen	slices of fresh strawberry
serves 2	(see page 4)	
	1 lb/450 g frozen forest fruits	
	(such as blueberries, raspberries,	
10 minutes	and blackberries)	
—		

Pour the orange juice into a food processor. Add the banana and half of the forest fruits and process until smooth.

Add the remaining forest fruits and process until smooth. Pour the mixture into tall glasses and decorate the rims with slices of fresh strawberry. Add straws and serve.

blueberry dazzler

		ingredients
extremely easy		
	³/₄ cup apple juice	DECORATION
serves 2	½ cup plain yogurt	whole fresh blueberries
	1 banana, sliced and frozen (see page 4)	
10 minutes	6 oz/175 g frozen blueberries	
—		

Pour the apple juice into a food processor. Add the yogurt and process until smooth.

Add the banana and half of the blueberries and process well, then add the remaining blueberries and process until smooth. Pour the mixture into tall glasses and add straws. Decorate with whole fresh blueberries and serve.

coconut cream

		ingredients	
very easy		1½ cups pineapple juice	DECORATION
		⅓ cup coconut milk	2 tbsp grated fresh coconut
serves 2		5½ oz/150 g vanilla ice cream	
		5 oz/140 g frozen pineapple chunks	TO SERVE
15 minutes			2 scooped-out coconut shells, optional
—			

Pour the pineapple juice and coconut milk into a food processor. Add the ice cream and process until smooth.

Add the pineapple chunks and process until smooth. Pour the mixture into scooped-out coconut shells, or tall glasses, and decorate with grated fresh coconut. Add straws and serve.

melon refresher

		ingredients	
extremely easy		1 cup plain yogurt	DECORATION
		3½ oz/100 g galia melon, cut	wedges of melon
serves 2		into chunks	
		3½ oz/100 g cantaloupe melon,	
		cut into chunks	
15 minutes		3½ oz/100 g watermelon, cut	
		into chunks	
		6 ice cubes	
—			

Pour the yogurt into a food processor. Add the galia melon chunks and process until smooth.

Add the cantaloupe and watermelon chunks along with the ice cubes and process until smooth. Pour the mixture into glasses and decorate with wedges of melon. Serve at once.

pineapple tango

		ingredients	
	extremely easy	½ cup pineapple juice	DECORATION
		juice of 1 lemon	wedges of fresh pineapple
	serves 2	scant ½ cup water	
		3 tbsp brown sugar	
		¾ cup plain yogurt	
	15 minutes	1 peach, cut into chunks and frozen	
		3½ oz/100 g frozen pineapple chunks	
	—		

Pour the pineapple juice, lemon juice, and water into a food processor. Add the sugar and yogurt and process until blended.

Add the peach and pineapple chunks and process until smooth. Pour the mixture into glasses and decorate the rims with wedges of fresh pineapple. Serve at once.

spiced apple smoothie

extremely easy		**ingredients**
	1 cup apple juice	DECORATION
	½ tsp powdered cinnamon	slices of fresh banana on
serves 2	2 tsp grated fresh root ginger	toothpicks
	2 bananas, sliced and frozen	
	(see page 4)	
15 minutes		
—		

Pour the apple juice into a food processor. Add the cinnamon and ginger and process gently until combined.

Add the bananas and process until smooth. Pour the mixture into tall glasses and add straws. Decorate with slices of fresh banana on toothpicks and serve.

breakfast smoothie

		ingredients	
	extremely easy	1 cup orange juice	DECORATION
		½ cup plain yogurt	slices of fresh banana
	serves 2	2 eggs	
		2 bananas, sliced and frozen (see page 4)	
	10 minutes		
	—		

Pour the orange juice and yogurt into a food processor and process gently until combined.

Add the eggs and frozen bananas and process until smooth. Pour the mixture into glasses and decorate the rims with slices of fresh banana. Add straws and serve.

orange & strawberry cream

extremely easy	
serves 2	
15 minutes	
—	

ingredients

¹/₂ cup plain yogurt
³/₄ cup strawberry yogurt
³/₄ cup orange juice
6 oz/175 g frozen strawberries
1 banana, sliced and frozen
  (see page 4)

DECORATION
slices of orange
whole fresh strawberries

Pour the plain and strawberry yogurts into a food processor and process gently. Add the orange juice and process until combined.

Add the strawberries and banana and process until smooth. Pour the mixture into tall glasses and decorate with slices of orange and whole strawberries. Add straws and serve.

vegan tropical smoothie

		ingredients	
extremely easy		scant ½ cup coconut milk	DECORATION
		generous ¾ cup soy milk	grated fresh coconut
serves 2		scant ½ cup pineapple juice	wedges of fresh pineapple
		1 tbsp brown sugar	
		1 ripe mango, pitted and diced	
		2 tbsp grated fresh coconut	
15 minutes		5 oz/140 g frozen pineapple chunks	
		1 banana, sliced and frozen	
—		(see page 4)	

Put the coconut milk, soy milk, pineapple juice, and sugar into a food processor and process gently until combined. Add the mango chunks to the food processor along with the grated coconut and process well.

Add the pineapple chunks and banana and process until smooth. Pour the mixture into glasses, scatter over some grated fresh coconut, and decorate the rims with wedges of fresh pineapple. Serve at once.

fig & maple melter

extremely easy	
serves 2	
15 minutes	
—	

ingredients

1½ cups hazelnut yogurt
2 tbsp freshly squeezed orange juice
4 tbsp maple syrup
8 large fresh figs, chopped
6 ice cubes

DECORATION
toasted chopped hazelnuts

Pour the yogurt, orange juice, and maple syrup into a food processor and process gently until combined.

Add the figs and ice cubes and process until smooth. Pour the mixture into glasses and scatter over some toasted chopped hazelnuts. Serve at once.

juices & slushes

Fruit and vegetable juices provide an instant supply of nutritional goodness: their life-giving benefits go straight into the body. The recipes in this chapter offer some exciting ideas, and after you have tried them, why not go on to experiment with your own combinations? The slushes, too, which you will find at the end of this chapter, are great revivers. They are especially refreshing on hot summer days.

tomato blazer

		ingredients	
extremely easy		generous 2 cups tomato juice dash of Worcestershire sauce 1 small red chile, seeded and chopped 1 scallion, trimmed and chopped 6 ice cubes	GARNISH 2 long, thin, red chiles, cut into flowers (see below)
serves 2			
15 minutes + 30 minutes to chill			
—			

To make the chile flowers, use a sharp knife to make six cuts along each chile. Place the point of the knife about ½ inch/1 cm from the stem end and cut toward the tip. Put the chiles in a bowl of iced water and let stand for about 25–30 minutes, until they have spread out into flower shapes.

Put the tomato juice and Worcestershire sauce into a food processor and process gently until combined. Add the chopped chile, scallion, and ice cubes, and process until smooth.

Pour the mixture into glasses and garnish with the chile flowers. Add straws and serve.

vegetable cocktail

		ingredients	
very easy		½ cup carrot juice	GARNISH
		1 lb 2 oz/500 g tomatoes, skinned,	2 celery stalks
serves 2		seeded, and coarsely chopped	
		1 tbsp lemon juice	
		4 celery stalks, trimmed and sliced	
15 minutes		4 scallions, trimmed and coarsely	
		chopped	
		1 oz/25 g fresh parsley	
—		1 oz/25 g fresh mint	

Put the carrot juice, tomatoes, and lemon juice into a food processor and process gently until combined.

Add the sliced celery along with the scallions, parsley, and mint, and process until smooth. Pour the mixture into glasses and garnish with celery stalks. Serve at once.

carrot & bell pepper booster

		ingredients
	extremely easy	1 cup carrot juice
		1 cup tomato juice
	serves 2	2 large red bell peppers, seeded and
		coarsely chopped
		1 tbsp lemon juice
	15 minutes	freshly ground black pepper
	—	

Pour the carrot juice and tomato juice into a food processor and process gently until combined.

Add the red bell peppers and lemon juice. Season with plenty of freshly ground black pepper and process until smooth. Pour the mixture into tall glasses, add straws, and serve.

curried vegetable juice

		ingredients	
	very easy	1 cup carrot juice	1 oz/25 g fresh parsley
		4 tomatoes, skinned, seeded, and	1 tsp curry powder
		coarsely chopped	6 ice cubes
	serves 2	1 tbsp lemon juice	1/2 cup water
		2 celery stalks, trimmed and sliced	
		1 romaine lettuce	GARNISH
	15 minutes	1 garlic clove, chopped	celery stalks
	—		

Put the carrot juice, tomatoes, lemon juice, and celery into a food processor and process gently until combined.

Separate the lettuce leaves, then wash them and add them to the food processor along with the garlic, parsley, curry powder, and ice cubes. Process until well combined, then pour in the water and process until smooth.

Pour the mixture into tall glasses and garnish with celery stalks. Serve at once.

carrot & ginger energizer

		ingredients	
	very easy	1 cup carrot juice	GARNISH
		4 tomatoes, skinned, seeded, and	chopped fresh parsley
	serves 2	coarsely chopped	
		1 tbsp lemon juice	
		1 oz/25 g fresh parsley	
	15 minutes	1 tbsp grated fresh root ginger	
		6 ice cubes	
		1/2 cup water	
	—		

Put the carrot juice, tomatoes, and lemon juice into a food processor and process gently until combined.

Add the parsley to the food processor along with the ginger and ice cubes. Process until well combined, then pour in the water and process until smooth.

Pour the mixture into glasses and garnish with chopped fresh parsley. Serve at once.

watercress & carrot juice

		ingredients	
extremely easy		generous 2 cups carrot juice 1 oz/25 g watercress (if unavailable you could use arugula or baby spinach instead) 1 tbsp lemon juice	GARNISH sprigs of fresh watercress, arugula, or baby spinach
serves 2			
10 minutes + 1 hour to chill			
—			

Pour the carrot juice into a food processor. Add the watercress and lemon juice and process until smooth. Transfer to a pitcher, cover with plastic wrap, and chill in the refrigerator for at least 1 hour, or until required.

When the mixture is thoroughly chilled, pour into glasses and garnish with sprigs of fresh watercress, arugula, or baby spinach. Serve at once.

cranberry sunrise

		ingredients
extremely easy	1¼ cups cranberry juice scant ½ cup orange juice 5½ oz/150 g fresh raspberries 1 tbsp lemon juice	DECORATION slices and spirals of fresh lemon or orange
serves 2		
10 minutes		
—		

Pour the cranberry juice and orange juice into a food processor and process gently until combined. Add the raspberries and lemon juice and process until smooth.

Pour the mixture into glasses and decorate with slices and spirals of fresh lemon or orange. Serve at once.

summer fruit slush

		ingredients	
	extremely easy	4 tbsp orange juice	DECORATION
		1 tbsp lime juice	fresh whole raspberries and
	serves 2	scant ½ cup sparkling water	blackberries on toothpicks
		12 oz/350 g frozen summer fruits	
		(such as blueberries, raspberries,	
	10 minutes	blackberries, and strawberries)	
		4 ice cubes	
	—		

Pour the orange juice, lime juice, and sparkling water into a food processor and process gently until combined.

Add the summer fruits and ice cubes and process until a slushy consistency has been reached.

Pour the mixture into glasses, decorate with whole raspberries and blackberries on toothpicks, and serve.

iced coffee & chocolate crush

		ingredients	
extremely easy		1³⁄₄ cups milk	DECORATION
		generous ³⁄₄ cup coffee syrup	grated chocolate
serves 2		scant ¹⁄₂ cup peppermint syrup	sprigs of fresh mint
		1 tbsp chopped fresh mint leaves	
		4 ice cubes	
15 minutes			
—			

Pour the milk, coffee syrup, and peppermint syrup into a food processor and process gently until combined.

Add the mint and ice cubes and process until a slushy consistency has been reached.

Pour the mixture into glasses. Scatter over the grated chocolate, decorate with sprigs of fresh mint, and serve.

melon & pineapple slush

	ingredients	
extremely easy	scant ½ cup pineapple juice	DECORATION
	4 tbsp orange juice	slices of galia melon
serves 2	4 oz/125 g galia melon, cut into chunks	slices of lemon
	5 oz/140 g frozen pineapple chunks	
10 minutes	4 ice cubes	
—		

Pour the pineapple juice and orange juice into a food processor and process gently until combined.

Add the melon, pineapple chunks, and ice cubes, and process until a slushy consistency has been reached.

Pour the mixture into glasses and decorate with slices of melon and lemon. Serve at once.

milkshakes

The milkshake has never lost its popularity. In fact, it seems to be more popular than ever. Milkshakes come in a wide variety of flavors and can be thick or not so thick, depending on the ratio of solid ingredients to milk. For example, many of them contain ice cream, and you can experiment with the thickness by varying the ratio of ice cream to liquid. You can also ring the changes by using a different flavor ice cream, or by substituting one type of fruit for another.

spiced banana milkshake

		ingredients
extremely easy		1¼ cups milk
		½ tsp allspice
serves 2		5½ oz/150 g banana ice cream
		2 bananas, sliced and frozen
		(see page 4)
10 minutes		
—		

Pour the milk into a food processor and add the allspice. Add half of the banana ice cream and process gently until combined, then add the remaining ice cream and process until well blended.

When the mixture is well combined, add the bananas and process until smooth. Pour the mixture into tall glasses, add straws, and serve at once.

coffee banana cooler

		ingredients
	extremely easy	1¼ cups milk
		4 tbsp instant coffee powder
	serves 2	5½ oz/150 g vanilla ice cream
		2 bananas, sliced and frozen
	10 minutes	(see page 4)
	—	

Pour the milk into a food processor, add the coffee powder, and process gently until combined. Add half of the vanilla ice cream and process gently, then add the remaining ice cream and process until well combined.

When the mixture is thoroughly blended, add the bananas and process until smooth. Pour the mixture into glasses and serve.

smooth nectarine shake

extremely easy	**ingredients**
	1 cup milk
	12 oz/350 g lemon sherbet
serves 2	1 ripe mango, pitted and diced
	2 ripe nectarines, pitted and diced
15 minutes	
—	

Pour the milk into a food processor, add half of the lemon sherbet, and process until combined. Add the remaining sherbet and process until smooth.

When the mixture is thoroughly blended, gradually add the mango and nectarines and process until smooth. Pour the mixture into glasses, add straws, and serve.

tropical storm

very easy	
serves 2	
15 minutes	
—	

ingredients

1 cup milk
scant ¼ cup coconut milk
5½ oz/150 g vanilla ice cream
2 bananas, sliced and frozen
  (see page 4)
7 oz/200 g canned pineapple chunks,
  drained
1 papaya, seeded and diced

DECORATION
grated fresh coconut
wedges of fresh pineapple

Pour the milk and coconut milk into a food processor and process gently until combined. Add half of the ice cream and process gently, then add the remaining ice cream and process until smooth.

Add the bananas and process well, then add the pineapple chunks and papaya and process until smooth. Pour the mixture into tall glasses, scatter over the grated coconut, and decorate the rims with pineapple wedges. Serve at once.

peach blush

		ingredients	
very easy		¾ cup milk	DECORATION
		8 oz/225 g canned peach slices,	fresh strawberries
serves 2		drained	
		2 fresh apricots, chopped	
		14 oz/400 g fresh strawberries, hulled	
20 minutes		and sliced	
		2 bananas, sliced and frozen	
		(see page 4)	
—			

Pour the milk into a food processor. Add the peach slices and process gently until combined. Add the apricots and process gently until combined.

Add the strawberries and banana slices and process until smooth. Pour the mixture into glasses and decorate the rims with fresh strawberries. Serve at once.

peach & orange milkshake

extremely easy	
serves 2	
15 minutes	
—	

ingredients

scant ½ cup milk
½ cup peach yogurt
scant ½ cup orange juice
8 oz/225 g canned peach slices, drained
6 ice cubes

DECORATION
strips of orange peel

Pour the milk, yogurt, and orange juice into a food processor and process gently until combined.

Add the peach slices and ice cubes and process until smooth. Pour the mixture into glasses and decorate with strips of orange peel. Add straws and serve.

chocolate milkshake

extremely easy	
serves 2	
10 minutes	
—	

ingredients

²/₃ cup milk

2 tbsp chocolate syrup

14 oz/400 g chocolate ice cream

DECORATION

grated chocolate

Pour the milk and chocolate syrup into a food processor and process gently until combined.

Add the chocolate ice cream and process until smooth. Pour the mixture into tall glasses and scatter over the grated chocolate. Serve at once.

creamy maple shake

		ingredients	
extremely easy		$^2/_3$ cup milk	DECORATION
		2 tbsp maple syrup	chopped almonds
serves 2		14 oz/400 g vanilla ice cream	
		1 tbsp almond extract	
15 minutes			
—			

Pour the milk and maple syrup into a food processor and process gently until combined.

Add the ice cream and almond extract and process until smooth. Pour the mixture into glasses and scatter over the chopped nuts. Add straws and serve.

peppermint refresher

extremely easy	
serves 2	
10 minutes	
—	

ingredients

²/₃ cup milk

2 tbsp peppermint syrup

14 oz/400 g peppermint ice cream

DECORATION

sprigs of fresh mint

Pour the milk and peppermint syrup into a food processor and process gently until combined.

Add the peppermint ice cream and process until smooth. Pour the mixture into tall glasses and decorate with sprigs of fresh mint. Add straws and serve.

kiwi & lime shake

		ingredients	
	extremely easy	²/₃ cup milk	DECORATION
		juice of 2 limes	slices of kiwifruit
	serves 2	2 kiwifruit, chopped	strips of lime peel
		1 tbsp sugar	
	15 minutes	14 oz/400 g vanilla ice cream	
	—		

Pour the milk and lime juice into a food processor and process gently until combined.

Add the chopped kiwis and sugar and process gently, then add the ice cream and process until smooth. Pour the mixture into glasses and decorate with slices of kiwifruit and strips of lime peel. Serve at once.

drinks for entertaining

The drinks in this chapter present a mouthwatering array of ingredients and flavors, from the stunning Mocha Cream— a feast of coffee, cream, and chocolate—to the delicately perfumed Lassi. These drinks will tantalize every palate, yet the good news is that they are alcohol-free, so everyone can enjoy them. You can make them as decorative as you like: suggestions for decoration have been given here, but feel free to experiment with your own.

mocha cream

		ingredients	
extremely easy		generous ¾ cup milk	DECORATION
		scant ¼ cup light cream	whipped cream
serves 2		1 tbsp brown sugar	grated chocolate
		2 tbsp unsweetened cocoa	
		1 tbsp coffee syrup or instant	
15 minutes		coffee powder	
		6 ice cubes	
—			

Put the milk, cream, and sugar into a food processor, and process gently until combined.

Add the unsweetened cocoa and coffee syrup or powder and process well, then add the ice cubes and process until smooth.

Pour the mixture into glasses. Top with whipped cream, scatter over the grated chocolate, and serve.

iced coffee with cream

		ingredients	
very easy			
		1³⁄₄ cups water	DECORATION
		2 tbsp instant coffee powder	light cream
serves 2		2 tbsp brown sugar	whole coffee beans
		6 ice cubes	
15 minutes + 1¼ hours to cool			
—			

Use the water and coffee powder to brew some hot coffee, then let cool to room temperature. Transfer to a pitcher, cover with plastic wrap, and chill in the refrigerator for at least 45 minutes.

When the coffee has chilled, pour it into a food processor. Add the sugar, and process until well combined. Add the ice cubes and process until smooth.

Pour the mixture into glasses. Float light cream on top, decorate with whole coffee beans, and serve.

coffee hazelnut soda

extremely easy	
serves 2	
15 minutes + 1¼ hours to cool	
—	

ingredients

1 cup water
3 tbsp instant coffee powder
½ cup sparkling water
1 tbsp hazelnut syrup
2 tbsp brown sugar
6 ice cubes

DECORATION
slices of lime
slices of lemon

Use the water and coffee powder to brew some hot coffee, then let cool to room temperature. Transfer to a pitcher, cover with plastic wrap, and chill in the refrigerator for at least 45 minutes.

When the coffee has chilled, pour it into a food processor. Add the sparkling water, hazelnut syrup, and sugar, and process well. Add the ice cubes and process until smooth.

Pour the mixture into glasses, decorate the rims with slices of fresh lime and lemon, and serve.

spiced lemon tea

		ingredients
extremely easy	1¾ cups water	DECORATION
	4 cloves	slices of lemon
serves 2	1 small stick of cinnamon	
	2 tea bags	
	3–4 tbsp lemon juice	
8–10 minutes	1–2 tbsp brown sugar	
3–4 minutes		

Put the water, cloves, and cinnamon stick into a pan and bring to a boil. Remove from the heat and add the tea bags. Let stand for 5 minutes to infuse, then remove the tea bags.

Stir in lemon juice and sugar to taste. Return the pan to the heat and warm through gently.

Remove the pan from the heat and strain the tea into heatproof glasses. Decorate with slices of lemon and serve.

iced citrus tea

		ingredients	
very easy	1 ¼ cups water	DECORATION	
	2 tea bags	wedge of lime	
serves 2	scant ½ cup orange juice	granulated sugar	
	4 tbsp lime juice	slices of orange, lemon or lime	
	1–2 tbsp brown sugar		
15 minutes + 1¼ hours to cool	8 ice cubes		
3–4 minutes			

Pour the water into a pan and bring to a boil. Remove from the heat, add the tea bags, and let stand for 5 minutes to infuse. Remove the tea bags and let the tea cool to room temperature (about 30 minutes). Transfer to a pitcher, cover with plastic wrap, and chill in the refrigerator for at least 45 minutes.

When the tea has chilled, pour in the orange juice and lime juice. Add sugar to taste.

Take two glasses and rub the rims with a wedge of lime, then dip them in granulated sugar to frost. Put the ice cubes into the glasses and pour over the tea. Decorate the rims with slices of fresh orange, lemon or lime and serve.

lassi

very easy	
serves 2	
15 minutes	
—	

ingredients

scant ½ cup plain yogurt
generous 2 cups milk
1 tbsp rose water
3 tbsp honey
1 ripe mango, pitted and diced
6 ice cubes

DECORATION
edible rose petals, optional

Pour the yogurt and milk into a food processor and process gently until combined.

Add the rose water and honey and process until thoroughly blended, then add the mango along with the ice cubes and process until smooth. Pour the mixture into glasses, decorate with edible rose petals, if using, and serve.

homemade lemonade

very easy	
serves 2	
15 minutes + 2½ hours to cool	
8–10 minutes	

ingredients

²/₃ cup water
6 tbsp sugar
1 tsp grated lemon zest
½ cup lemon juice
6 ice cubes

TO SERVE
sparkling water

DECORATION
wedge of lemon
granulated sugar
slices of lemon

Put the water, sugar, and lemon zest into a small pan and bring to a boil, stirring constantly. Continue to boil, stirring, for 5 minutes.

Remove from the heat and let cool to room temperature. Stir in the lemon juice, then transfer to a pitcher, cover with plastic wrap, and chill in the refrigerator for at least 2 hours.

When the lemonade has almost finished chilling, take two glasses and rub the rims with a wedge of lemon, then dip them in granulated sugar to frost. Put the ice cubes into the glasses.

Remove the lemon syrup from the refrigerator, pour it over the ice, and top up with sparkling water. The ratio should be one part lemon syrup to three parts sparkling water. Stir well to mix, decorate with slices of fresh lemon, and serve.

cherry soda

extremely easy	
serves 2	
5 minutes	
—	

ingredients

8 ice cubes, crushed

2 tbsp cherry syrup

generous 2 cups sparkling water

DECORATION

maraschino cherries on toothpicks

Divide the crushed ice between two tall glasses and pour over the cherry syrup.

Top up each glass with sparkling water. Decorate with the maraschino cherries on toothpicks and serve.

pineapple float

		ingredients	
easy	¾ cup pineapple juice	TO SERVE
	⅓ cup coconut milk	2 scooped-out pineapple shells,
serves 2	7 oz/200 g vanilla ice cream	optional
	5 oz/140 g frozen pineapple chunks	
15–20 minutes	¾ cup sparkling water	
—		

Pour the pineapple juice and coconut milk into a food processor. Add the ice cream and process until smooth.

Add the pineapple chunks and process well. Pour the mixture into scooped-out pineapple shells or tall glasses, until two-thirds full. Top up with sparkling water, add straws, and serve.

raspberry & apple quencher

		ingredients
extremely easy	8 ice cubes, crushed 2 tbsp raspberry syrup generous 2 cups chilled apple juice	DECORATION whole raspberries and pieces of apple on toothpicks
serves 2		
5 minutes		
—		

Divide the crushed ice between two glasses and pour over the raspberry syrup.

Top up each glass with chilled apple juice and stir well. Decorate with the whole raspberries and pieces of apple on toothpicks and serve at once.

carrot & orange cream

extremely easy	
serves 2	
10 minutes	
—	

ingredients

¾ cup carrot juice
¾ cup orange juice
5½ oz/150 g vanilla ice cream
6 ice cubes

DECORATION
slices of orange
strips of orange peel

Pour the carrot juice and orange juice into a food processor and process gently until well combined. Add the ice cream and process until thoroughly blended.

Add the ice and process until smooth. Pour the mixture into glasses, decorate with slices of orange and strips of orange peel, and serve.

index